I0151631

Stepping
Into Growth
A Workbook of 7 Strategies to a Godly Self-Esteem

Lisa Cassman

Halo
PUBLISHING
INTERNATIONAL

Copyright © 2022 Lisa Cassman
Bible translation the scripture is from: NIV
Edited by: Leah Kelton
Photos edited by: Leah Kelton
Dedication Photos by: Leah Shellum
Headshot by: Mariah Geoghegan
Cover Photo and Content Photos by: Lisa Cassman
All rights reserved.

No part of this book may be reproduced in any manner
whatsoever without the prior written permission of the publisher,
except in the case of brief quotations embodied in reviews.

The views and opinions expressed in this book are those of
the author and do not necessarily reflect the official policy or
position of Halo Publishing International. Any content provided
by our authors are of their opinion and are not intended to
malign any religion, ethnic group, club, organization, company,
individual or anyone or anything.

ISBN: 978-1-63765-185-8
LCCN: 2022902212

Halo
PUBLISHING
INTERNATIONAL

Halo Publishing International, LLC
www.halopublishing.com

Printed and bound in the United States of America

To my husband Steve, our grandchildren, and all their parents! Thank you for being a blessing in my life.

"I praise you because I am fearfully and wonderfully made; your works are wonderful, I know that full well."
— Psalm 139:14

"Be kind and compassionate to one another, forgiving each other, just as in Christ God forgave you."
— Eph. 4:32

Contents

Introduction   **11**

**Journaling Questions to Start
us on our Journey**   **13**

Section One: **27**

How to Take Control of Your
Life Once and For All

   1. What is Anxiety?   27

   2. Do You Procrastinate?   32

   3. Nothing in Life is Perfect   35

   4. Don't let Fear Rule your Life   38

Section Two: **41**

How to Quiet the Inner Critic that Causes
you to Make the Wrong Decisions

   5. What Is Self-Esteem?   41

   6. Caterpillar to Butterfly   45

Section Three: 48

Ways to Let Go of the Hurt and Emotional Pain, so you can Move Forward with Hope and Happiness

7. What is Forgiveness?   48
8. God's Word Tells us to Forgive   51
9. We can Forgive Ourselves   53
10. Forgiveness does not Always mean Reconciliation   56

Section Four: 58

Simple Action Steps you can use Right Now to Increase your Self-Esteem

11. Don't React in Hurt   58
12. What is stress?   61
13. Symptoms of Stress Overload   65
14. Coping with Stress   68
15. Using our Hurts as Room for Growth   70

Section Five: 72

The One Thing you Absolutely Need to find Love and Happiness

16. Cold Heart   72
17. Restoring the House   75
18. Victory   78

Section Six: 81

What Does God Say About You?

19. How do you Choose to Love?   81
20. Looking in the Mirror   84
21. God's Love   87

Section Seven: 89

Prayer for Healing

22. Finding Joy and Holding onto it 89
23. Lay It at the Cross   92
24. Encouragement   94

Journaling Space   96

Introduction

"This is the day the Lord has made,
let us rejoice and be glad in it."
– Psalm 118: 24

Look into the greatest gift— God's love!

Take a moment to answer the questions on the next few pages before getting started with the rest of the workbook.

Really focus on processing through your answers. This is a self-help book to allow you to move into finding yourself and who God created you to be and, in the process, allowing you to heal relationships, improve self-esteem, see value in yourself and find deep, abiding self-worth.

"Trust in the Lord with all your heart and lean not on your own understanding; in all your ways acknowledge Him, and He will make your paths straight" (Proverb 3:5-6).

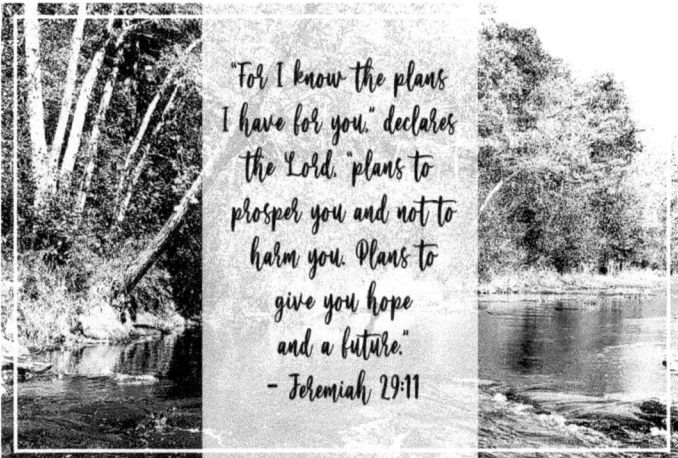

"For I know the plans I have for you," declares the Lord, "plans to prosper you and not to harm you. Plans to give you hope and a future."
– Jeremiah 29:11

Journaling Questions to Start us on our Journey

My favorite childhood memory / memories…

When I think about my childhood,
what I miss the most…

Was there something from your childhood that
you would have changed if you could?

If I could change one thing about
my life now it would be...

The one thing I regret in life is…

Something that was special to
me as a child that I miss is...

Something I tried and failed at...

My greatest heartbreak…

My greatest failure…

The last time I felt happy…

The last time I felt sad…

I felt in control when I…

_____

_____

_____

_____

_____

_____

_____

_____

_____

_____

_____

_____

_____

The one thing I want to change about myself…

Section One:

How to Take Control of Your Life Once and For All

I lift up my eyes to mountains--
where does my help come from?
My help comes from the Lord,
the maker of heaven and earth."
-- Psalm 121:1-2

1. What is Anxiety?

What is anxiety and what can cause it?

Anxiety is a feeling of worry or nervousness brought on by not understanding what the outcome of a situation may be. If you are overworked, that too can cause anxiety attacks. If you haven't had enough sleep or you worry about what the future will bring-- maybe not knowing if you will have a job, or enough money. Stress and anxiety go hand in hand.

Symptoms of anxiety may include:

- Worrying about the future.

- Physically Shaking.

- Headaches or body aches.

- Sweating, rapid heartbeat, weakness.

What can you do to control an anxiety attack?

- Take a deep breath. Take a moment for your-self and do some stretches or a few minutes of mediation.

- You can also get yourself a red light and sit with soft music for a little bit.

- Go for a walk, slowly. Don't over stimulate yourself.

- Try not to be in the dark— you will need light. Walk outside in the sunlight if you can.

Basically, anxiety can happen when you rely on your own strength instead of God's.

Journal your Thoughts:

When you're experiencing anxiety, what is something you can do differently than what you would normally do? Why do you think that could work?

What would you tell someone else with the same issue you have?

Try to think of something else besides the same thing that has caused you to have the attack, something positive. What would that one thing be?

2. Do You Procrastinate?

Do you procrastinate? What are some reasons you may procrastinate?

Maybe you don't know how to start the task, or the task is too large. Some may even find the task too boring. What is the reason you are doing this task? Is it something you feel you need to do or is it for someone else?

If it is something that absolutely needs to get done, take the time to look at it from all angles and work at it to finish. If it is too large, break it into smaller steps to work on it. Set yourself a deadline for its completion, but set yourself a smaller deadline too, within the task, so you won't keep putting it off.

Journal your Thoughts:

What is it you want to do? Is it attainable?

Is there someone you would like to connect with in the near future? Who is it, and how do you plan to connect? By Phone, letter, email, maybe a visit? Plan how you will proceed here.

3. Nothing in Life is Perfect

Many people with anxiety may have unrealistic expectations about themselves and others. People suffer from not reaching an understanding of their own inner being, but they may also experience distress in a host of social situations based on who they think they're supposed to be; meaning, perfect.

Sometimes we think others are supposed to be perfect, to never do anything wrong. Maybe it's that you are expecting a job to be perfect while coming to realize there are some things that are too hard for you to do, or you have to work longer days than you had been told. There can be things everyday that go wrong but how will you handle it?

Example: A pastor making a bad choice because he is having a bad day, but he is also human and will make mistakes. Or maybe someone wants to have a baby to have someone to love her, instead of her having a baby to love. The child may grow up angry and bitter because of the selfish reasons for which they were brought into the world.

Don't set yourself up for failure by expecting people to be perfect, including children and parents.

Journal your Thoughts:

Can you name some situations right now that you know you are having a hard time with because it is different from what you had expected?

What can you do to change the situation by changing the way you think about it?

4. Don't let Fear Rule your Life

What do you fear? Fear can be triggered by many different things or life events.

We don't know what life is going to bring us or where it will take us. The fears affecting your life now could be because something has happened in your past. Like maybe your home starting on fire from a lightning storm so you are now scared of storms. Or someone you loved was in a car accident so you are afraid to travel too far. It could be something as small as being afraid of spiders or snakes, but the fear feels so big to the one frightened.

God's Word tell us, "Peace I leave with you; my peace I give you. I do not give to you as the world gives. Do not let your hearts be troubled and do not be afraid" (John 14:27). It even gives us a roadmap for dealing with our fears when they have us in their clutches: "I sought the Lord, and he answered me; he delivered me from all my fears" (Psalm 34:4).

Journal your Thoughts:

What are you afraid of? What has happened in your life that produced that fear in you? What can you do to change it now?

Describe a recent situation where you avoided rather than faced and embraced your fear. It could be at work or in a relationship or anywhere you had to face it.

How to Quiet the Inner Critic that Causes you to Make the Wrong Decisions

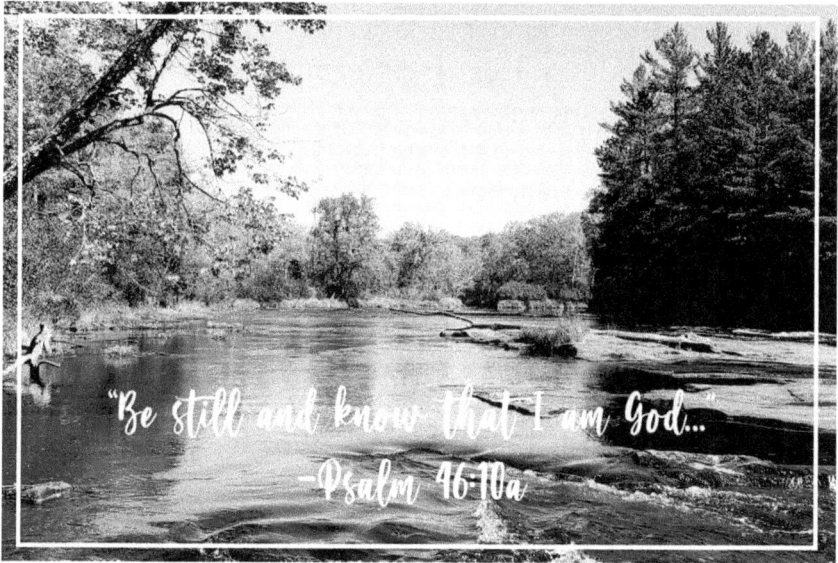

"Be still and know that I am God..."
—Psalm 46:10a

5. What Is Self-Esteem?

While doing inner work on yourself, you can see your self-esteem being built up.

What is self-esteem? The way one sees oneself, whether emotionally or physically; judging what one can or cannot do.

Don't depend on others for your self-worth; only you can change how you feel and think. You are responsible for your own actions and how you react to what happens to you. We all like to have others notice us and notice what we have done and like to have someone tell us "great job." Many times we may look for satisfaction from others, and the positive feedback that we so long for. As soon as someone close to you, who has been a special influence in your life, hurts you or turns their back on you, then you may start the negative self-talk even if you know deep down that you're happy with yourself and what you have made of your life. We have such a tendency not to accept constructive criticism or negative feedback from people. You can turn right back to where you first were, where you don't feel like you have accomplished anything. We all appreciate compliments but shouldn't live our lives by them.

Give yourself credit for being you. None of us are perfect, but we also know that Jesus died for us, because He loves us so much (John 3:16). Stay true to yourself and remember that God made you special. Self-esteem is not just feeling good about yourself, but rather accepting what you don't do or what you can't do.

Keep your head up and appear confident. Tell yourself you ARE good enough. Talk positive; throw out the negative. While you can be proud of yourself, don't overdo it with being haughty or over-bearing. You may risk falling backwards or hurting others in the process.

It is okay to have setbacks, but we shouldn't feel like a failure because life isn't perfect and we can't expect it to be. If you make a mistake, it's okay. Try again. There will be circumstances that will drag you down. You get to bring yourself back up again.

If someone has hurt you, remember it isn't your fault. Their behavior is their choice. Your choice is how you handle and react to it.

Look at the brighter side! Find a reason to smile. Remember that life is fun. What were things like before you felt this way? Read a joke book, listen to Christian comedy. Keep in contact with your sense of humor. Worrying and dwelling on the negative just allows you to create more problems for yourself and makes things more complicated. God wants our worries and all our baggage.

Weed out the negative thoughts and irrational feelings. Work towards a goal but make sure it's a realistic one to keep staying ahead of yourself and keeping it positive so you won't knock yourself down. Tell yourself you are worth it and you won't allow anyone to tell you otherwise.

Now go stand by the mirror and tell yourself "I am worth it!"

Journal your Thoughts:

Do you feel like you have a healthy self-esteem? Which of the areas mentioned here do you think would be most helpful for you to work on in order to help your self-esteem reach its full potential?

6. Caterpillar to Butterfly

Remember the caterpillar turns into a beautiful butterfly.

Sometimes when we are about to give up, and we least expect it, life throws us something wonderful and we just have to acknowledge it and see the true beauty in what it is and where it has come from. Maybe an unexpected gift or gesture from someone; something so minor or as unexpected as someone paying for the items you were going to purchase anyway, or someone complimenting you on what you're wearing.

Focus on the positive and on all that you have accomplished instead of dwelling on the what-ifs and the negatives.

"May the God of hope fill you with all joy and peace as you trust in him, so that you may overflow with hope by the power of the Holy Spirit" (Romans 15:13).

Journal your Thoughts:

Take time to write a list of the positive things that have made an impact on your life. Did any just happen or was there some role you played in making it happen?

Think about how one of these positive things changed you as a person and did it make an impact on anyone else's life?

Section Three:

Ways to Let Go of the Hurt and Emotional Pain, so you can Move Forward with Hope and Happiness

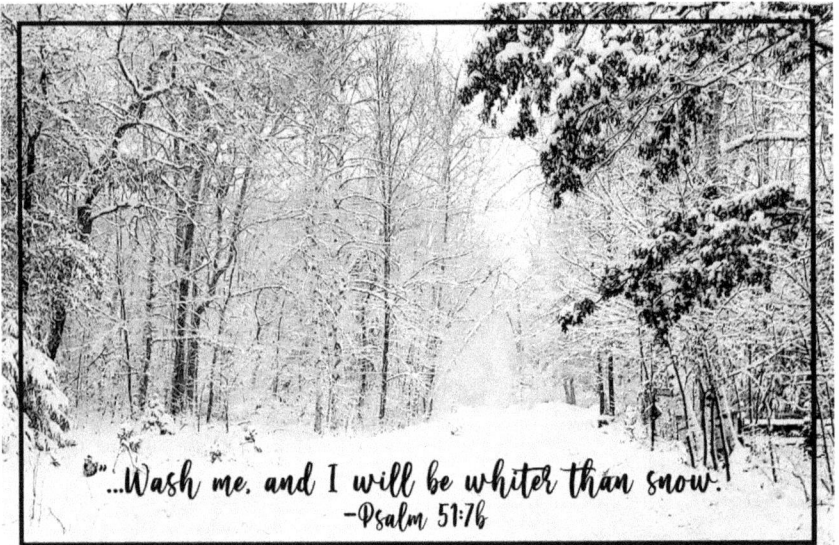

"...Wash me, and I will be whiter than snow."
—Psalm 51:7b

7. What is Forgiveness?

Forgiveness is turning away from our old life of sin and a conscious decision to let go of anger or resentment toward a person who has hurt you. It doesn't mean that you have forgotten or excused the behavior. It means you have made a decision to let go of the pain. You don't have to reconcile with the person in question, and it may take time before your feelings fall in line with your conscious decision.

Forgiveness is a choice. it's not that we can't forgive, we choose not to. It is an emotion that we choose to feel. Your heart may be so bitter, and your emotions so hurt, that you may tell yourself that you don't want to forgive the one who has hurt you. But do you want this person or situation to continually control your life? That's what happens when you choose to continue hanging on to the hurt and pain.

Here are some ways to help you forgive someone who has hurt you:

- Understand why it happened.

- Avoid focusing on the feelings directed at the person who hurt you.

- Check yourself for the times you have hurt someone else.

- Talk to God and ask for Him to help you let go.

- Write a letter to the person that has hurt you telling them what they have done to hurt you and how it made you feel, and read it out loud into the mirror.

- Tell the person you have forgiven them.

Journal your Thoughts:

Write a list of people you need to forgive and what they did that you have been holding on to.

8. God's Word Tells us to Forgive

Imagine the moment you gave your life to Christ and he instantly forgave you. He didn't say, "Wait until I let go of the heartache you caused me."

We don't want to forgive those who have hurt us because we just want to hang on to the hurt for a while still.

His love is so great and we really don't deserve the love and forgiveness he chooses to give us, but he forgives us over and over again.

Even if the other person hasn't asked us to forgive them, we still have the obligation to move forward with God's love in us. Love conquers all. Not just for the person you are forgiving, but for you.

God's word tells us to forgive:

- Jesus says if the son sets you free you are free indeed (John 8:36).

- Forgive so the father will forgive you (Matthew 6:14).

- Forgive as the Lord forgave you (Colossians 3:13).

We may not always feel like the one who has hurt us deserves it, but none of us do. His love is so unconditional and worthy for us to walk in His footsteps. We have a great, big, wonderful God who loves all of us so much that he deserves our praise and worship.

Journal your Thoughts:

Express your gratitude to God for all the things He's forgiven you of. Sometimes when we realize how deep His mercy is for us, it's easier to muster some mercy of our own for others.

9. We can Forgive Ourselves

We all make mistakes and choices that we may regret in life. So much so that we have hurt others in the process. We can also learn to forgive ourselves from the pain we have caused.

Here's how:

- Accept responsibility for what you have done; don't blame someone else for your choices. Sometimes you may do things because you are afraid and you don't want someone to have the power to hurt you if you don't make that particular choice. But you still need to realize that it was, in the end, your decision.

- Make amends. Let the person you have hurt know that you would like to apologize. Say you are sorry and let them know that you feel remorse. Then change your behavior.

- Allow yourself to learn and grow. Come to understand why you have made the choices you have, and that will help keep you from doing it in the future.

Do not judge, do not condemn, forgive and you will be forgiven (Luke 6:37).

Journal your Thoughts:

Is there someone in your life you would like to ask to forgive you? How can you change your behavior so it doesn't happen again?

Be honest with yourself, do you sometimes hurt people before they have a chance to hurt you?

10. Forgiveness does not Always mean Reconciliation

Forgiveness doesn't mean you have to forget about the pain and hurt caused by others; it takes time. Once you are able to forgive others and yourself you can take baby steps to trust again, crushing the enemy, rising up with Christ and allowing your heart to heal.

God says to love and pray for your enemy (Matthew 5:43-48). We let our hearts become so hurt that we allow ourselves to hurt others in the process.

Remember that even on a cloudy day, you can find sunshine. Life is beautiful, you just have to find the beauty in it. Know that there is life after being hurt. The rainbow is a beautiful example of life after a storm.

Some ways you know that your trust has been broken with someone:

- You feel overly jealous over every little thing.

- You are expecting them to hurt you because of your experience of them in the past.

- You notice they tell lies about someone.

Some ways you can be too trusting:

- You won't listen to others who warn you that something's up.

- You believe stories that are outrageous from the person you're being warned about.

Journal your Thoughts:

Do you think you tend to be mistrustful in your relation-ships or too trusting? What are some of the symptoms you notice in your own relationships?

Section Four:

Simple Action Steps you can use Right Now to Increase your Self-Esteem

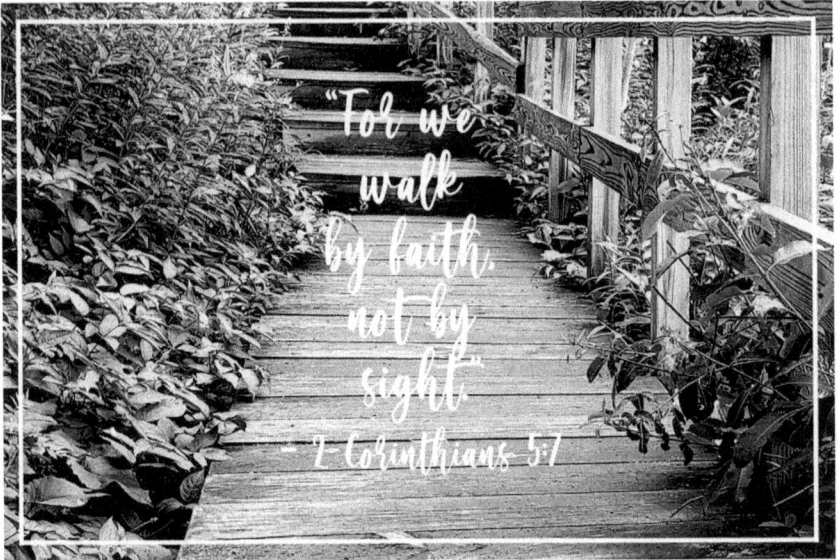

"For we walk by faith, not by sight."
– 2 Corinthians 5:7

11. Don't React in Hurt

The saying, 'When life throws you lemons, make lemonade', isn't always as easy as it sounds.

Life may lead us on many detours, but God still always knows the way for us. He will guide anyone who is willing to follow Him. He gives us each free will to decide the choices we make and how we choose to react to what may happen that we have no control over— whether we follow Him or we choose not to.

58

God will not force us to do what He would like for us. He is such a loving God that He loves us unconditionally and will still love us and hold us no matter what life choices we make. He may be hurt and not liking the decisions we are making but He is still there for us. Even if we walk away from Him.

He will never lead us astray or into temptation.

We have a tendency to view things differently from how God may view them. For example, if someone does something to hurt us, we may hang onto it for quite some time and feel the world owes us because we have been hurt. We hold onto the pain until it damages us with anxiety or stress, which then can lead to our feelings being so hurt that it eventually causes physical issues.

When we are hurting we can easily hurt others in the process by saying things we shouldn't and causing pain to others. Our tongue can be used as such a deadly weapon, more than any other part of the body. Gossip or just saying mean things to one another can cause a spark which can lead to a huge wildfire. No human being can tame the tongue (James 3:6-8).

Journal your Thoughts:

Can you think of ways that you have hurt others as a reaction to your own hurt? How can you keep from doing this again?

12. What is stress?

What is stress and what causes it?

Stress is a mental or emotional strain or tension resulting from a demanding circumstance.

Stress can be caused by:

- **Lack of self-worth**: If something has happened in your life that you have no control over to cause low self-worth, you may be dwelling on the negative things around you. Something may trigger the trauma and, mentally, you go back to when it happened. Take care of yourself and get enough sleep. Keep up with your hair and personal hygiene. Do something productive like going for a walk, exercise or read a book that you enjoy.

- **Unrealistic perfectionism or expectations of oneself or another person**: Don't think you always have to be right or be perfect. Learn to be content and remember, "I can do all things through Christ who strengthens me." Don't try to do everything on your own guidance.

- **Your Boundaries have been broken**: Someone came inside your bubble and you can't let go of the pain and hurt they caused you. Share your stress with someone that you can trust. Talking about it puts it into perspective. Maybe you could join a group where others have had similar experiences.

Journal your Thoughts:

Brainstorm here three ideas of ways you can take care of yourself when your feelings of low self-worth are triggered:

What are some areas where you think you may have unrealistic expectations of yourself?

Think about who might be safe to talk to about the times your boundaries have been disrespected and what you'd like to process aloud to them:

13. Symptoms of Stress Overload

Symptoms of stress overload can be many things. For example:

- Making decisions might be unreasonably difficult, both major and minor ones. Whether it is buying something as small as a pair of shoes or as major as a house.

- You might have paranoid ideas of mistrust from family and friends.

- You might be over-thinking things that have happened or haven't; dwelling on a fear of what could happen.

- Frequent outbursts or unusual behavior. You might be making choices that you wouldn't normally— and hurting others in the process.

- Daydreaming about getting away from it all and being alone.

Journal your Thoughts:

Do you see yourself reflected in any of these symptoms currently? Have you in the past?

What are some events that have caused you stress in your life? Are you ready to put that stress aside? And how do you plan on accomplishing that?

14. Coping with Stress

How can you cope with stress?

- Know your limits! If you can't change a problem, don't fight what you have no control over. Learn to accept what it is until it has changed.

- It is okay to cry; we all need to show our emotions. Holding in the hurt may make things harder for yourself.

- Make time for fun.

Remember, "I can do all things through Christ who strengthens me" (Philippians 4:13).

Journal your Thoughts:

Can you brainstorm some more ways to cope with stress in your life?

15. Using our Hurts as Room for Growth

While we find life to be quite a challenge at times, we put on our blinders to what others are really going through.

There was a time when I was very hurt and couldn't find a way to let go and move forward. I found myself talking about one of the other young moms behind her back. I used my own pain as an excuse, and I gossiped about others also.

I knew it was wrong. She was hurting and I needed to be there for her. It was when she sought me out to tell me that I was one of the only people who didn't judge her for her life choices that I had a quick awakening and had to ask God to show me the truth about myself. I didn't want to know what He had to reveal, but it led to more freedom for me as I learned to let go of my judgmental thoughts and unkind behaviors over this woman.

Journal your Thoughts:

Is there someone in your life that God might be trying to use to wake you up to your own unhealthy, unkind, and sinful behaviors? Ask Him to convict and instruct and grow you now.

Section Five:

The One Thing you Absolutely Need to find Love and Happiness

"In all your ways acknowledge him. and he will make your paths straight."
- Proverbs 3:5-6

16. Cold Heart

Sometimes life sucks.

Our hearts can be cold, unchangeable, unbendable. It seems that no matter what we do everything goes wrong. We become frustrated and sometimes angry. Sometimes we want to blame others for our problems or situations. But at some point everyone must "own up" and accept their responsibilities.

Maybe you have tried and can't do it on your own. You need help, God can help. He can bring you the change you need. You must be willing to accept that sometimes change hurts before there is healing. You must let go of control and give it to Him. You must be willing to consciously work at it. God loves you; God is love. His love is perfect. God has the tools needed to change your heart.

We don't feel worthy once we've chosen to walk away from God's love. We can't always see that God still loves us.

I once met a man who was raised in church and due to unforeseen circumstances, he allowed himself to walk away from God and learn witchcraft. While chatting with him, he talked about how he has no interest in God. One thing that stands out in my memory is him asking me, "Aren't you going to tell me I'm going to hell?" I let him know that I am not his judge. That's not my place; it is between him and God.

No matter how anyone lives it's not up to us to say if that person will be with God. Only God himself can see that.

In the end, this man asked me to pray for him. Perhaps it was the beginning of a journey back into the love of God which is simply waiting for him with arms wide open.

Journal your Thoughts:

Are there ways in which you have turned your face away from God and now don't feel like you can turn back? Write a prayer here asking Him to show you the way, and/or write down a few people whom you might ask to pray for you on this journey.

17. Restoring the House

Picture an old, abandoned house that has wonderful characteristics. It may have broken windows, chipped paint, shutters falling off, doors broken and hanging wide open. Think about what kind of family once lived there. Was it a happy family with wonderful memories? Or was it a broken family which was very unhappy and not living the dream they had once worked so hard for.

This house needs attention, lots of work, and we can't just cover up the old paint or shut the door on its broken hinges expecting it to close again. We need to get to the bones of it and work hard to restore it. It could take months or years.

This is just like with old wounds; it takes time to heal and move forward. What are your heartaches that stick with you? What has caused them and what was your life like before it happened?

Journal your Thoughts:

Write your story from the beginning to now (using more paper if you have to). It doesn't have to be a masterpiece but get it down on paper. As you write, think about why you're choosing to share the events you have chosen and leave out others. Explain here why you think these events have been most impactful in your life?

Thinking about your story, did you grow up going to church? How was your life impacted by attending church and do you still attend? Where does God stand in your life right now?

18. Victory

Life can take twists and turns and tell you that you aren't worth it, but you can choose to tell yourself that you are valuable and know that victory over the negative sense of self is in sight. When you get through it all, you will be blessed, knowing that you are stronger than you ever thought. You just have to believe it!

Today, go to the mirror and smile, telling yourself that you are valuable and there is victory in sight! Knowing that you are just a step away from liking who and what you are.

"And you shall know the truth and the truth shall set you free" (John 8:32).

Journal your Thoughts:

Think about what your 90-year-old self would know about whom you were at a younger age? Describe what you think may be in your eulogy...

Do you want God or satan to have the final say in your life? What promises have you made to God? Have you kept them?

Section Six:

What Does God Say About You?

"For the Lord God is a sun and a shield; the Lord bestows favor and honor; no good thing does he withhold from those whose walk is blameless."
– Psalm 84:11

19. How do you Choose to Love?

To love is to have deep affection for, strong feelings. God loves us so much. Turn to His ways, not your own, and He will teach you to love like He does. He could let us be on our own, but he is greater than life and he wants us to be in peace and have grace.

You tell yourself, "I can't forgive myself," but He says, "I forgive you" (1 John 1:9).

You tell yourself, "I can't do it," but He says, "I can do all things" (Philippians 4:13).

You tell yourself, "Nobody cares for me," but He says, "I care for you" (1 Peter 5:17).

You tell yourself, "Nobody really loves me," but He says, "I love you" (John 3:16).

You tell yourself, "It's impossible," but He says, "All things are possible with Me" (Luke 18:27).

You tell yourself, "I am too tired," and He says, "I will give you rest" (Matthew 11:28).

Journal your Thoughts:

Which declarations that God makes do you find it more difficult to accept in your own life? What do you think would change in the way that you live if you began to take Him at His word?

20. Looking in the Mirror

Take a moment to describe what you look like. Do you like what you are describing? What do you like the least about your physical description, and what do you like the most?

Now remind yourself of what you like the most about your entire self, not just your physical self. What do you feel you are worth?

Use this exercise to train yourself that you are worth something.

1. For the next 3 consecutive days, pause to really look in the mirror once a day.

2. Really look in your eyes and into your heart to focus on the real you, not just your physical attributes. Look deep down into yourself and into your well-being.

3. Write notes to yourself of positive things you see and put them on the mirror to remind yourself.

"I have told you these things so that in me you may have peace. In this world you will have trouble, but take heart! I have overcome the world" (John 16:33).

"Anyone who listens to the word but does not do what it says is like a someone who looks at his face in a mirror, and after observing himself goes away and immediately forgets what he looks like" (James 1:23).

Journal Your Thoughts:

What are some of your accomplishments in your life? Describe in detail.

What are some positive things that have happened in your life because of them?

21. God's Love

God loves you so much. He wants you to know it, so He gave you His son so you can live.

You may have issues from your past but letting go of them, you can learn to love who you are now and what life has to offer. Will you be disappointed at times? Yes! Is life going to be perfect? Absolutely not. But you can make the best of what you have and what you have done. You can take the disappointments and use them for the good of others. Someone else may have been through some of the same sort of things that you have and they need your encouragement.

Practice the gift of love, tell yourself that you love who you are and who God created you to be.

"Love prospers when a fault is forgiven, but dwelling on it separates close friends" (Proverbs 17:9).

"For He has rescued us from the dominion of darkness and brought us into the kingdom of the son He loves, in whom we have redemption, the forgiveness of sins" (Colossians 1:13-14).

"Dear friends, lets us love one another, for love comes from God. Everyone who loves has been born of God and knows God" (1 John 4:7).

Journal your Thoughts:

Look up some other scripture on love and forgiveness and share the reference and what the scripture means to you here.

Section Seven:

Prayer for Healing

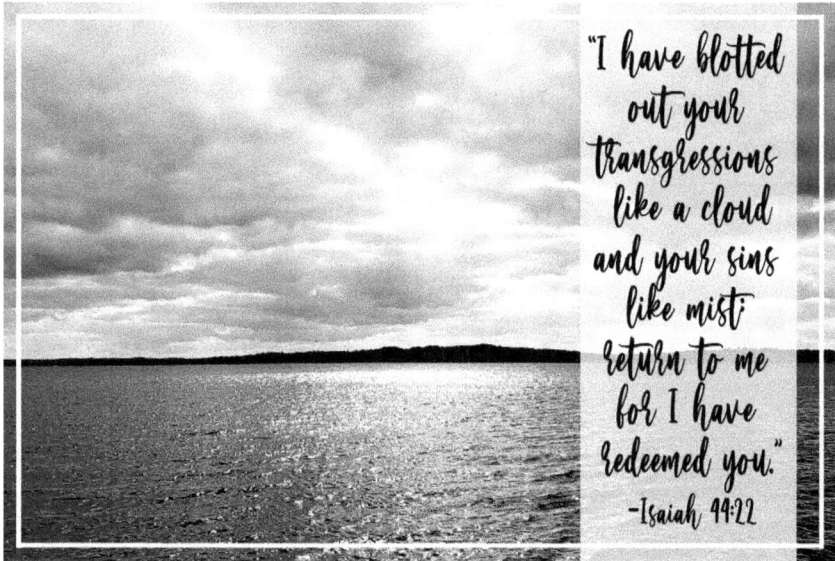

"I have blotted out your transgressions like a cloud and your sins like mist; return to me for I have redeemed you."
—Isaiah 44:22

22. Finding Joy and Holding onto it

"Weeping may last for the night, but joy comes in the morning" (Psalm 30:5).

Maybe you have lost your job, your marriage has ended, or you have lost a loved one. Whatever you have lost, know that God has His way and His timing to help you through your trials. You may not feel God's love for a while when all of a sudden something comes up that makes you know your life is changed for the better.

The best is yet to come. You may have taken life too seriously and allowed the little things to get in the way of finding the joy you deserve. Nobody is in charge of your happiness except you. Live your life to the fullest and find what you like to do.

There is hope no matter what has happened or what you may have done. Eventually your days will look better.

"I sought the Lord and He answered me and delivered me from all my fears. Those who look to Him are radiant, and their faces shall never be ashamed. This poor man cried, and the Lord heard him and saved him out of His troubles" (Psalm 34:4-6).

Journal your Thoughts:

Can you think of a time in your past when you had suffered great loss, and then the 'joy that came in your morning'? Describe it and take courage that the morning always comes after the dark of night.

23. Lay It at the Cross

What do you need healing from? We seem to know when to pray for healing when it comes to a physical illness but when it is an emotional suffering we tend to have a harder time letting it go and giving it to God.

There are many different forms of tragedies that can hit us. Some may come in a slow form and others can come unexpected, but they both hit us hard. Either way, God doesn't want us to carry our burdens. He wants to take them to the cross that He died on so we don't have to be so broken-hearted.

What is your emotional heartache you are carrying? It might be from the trauma of physical harm or abuse, childhood abuse or neglect, natural disaster trauma, home fire or other home loss, job loss and unemployment, financial crash, sudden and unexpected death of a loved one, serious illness, traumatic accident, or many others...

These can cause PTSD (Post Traumatic Stress Disorder) if not treated and worked on.

God's Word says, "'But I will restore you to health and heal your wounds,' declares the Lord" (Jeremiah 30:17). And promises, "He heals the brokenhearted and binds up their wounds" (Psalm 147:3).

Journal your Thoughts:

How can you open your heart to God today? If He told you today you don't have to hurt anymore, would you give it to Him? Why or why not?

24. Encouragement

Who has hurt you? Are you still holding on to the hurt, and thereby letting that person control you? How about a situation that has happened in your life that is controlling you?

Take a moment to write a letter to the person on your mind who has hurt you. Afterwards, take it and read it out loud to yourself.

Who or what gives you joy? Who are your positive influences in your life? Who has encouraged you the most? I encourage you to take a moment to write a letter to that person and let her/him know that. Go ahead and send this one.

Who can you encourage that maybe is hurting because of something that has happened in their life?

You get to take the victory and live your life to the fullest.

Journal your Thoughts:

Write your two letters, one to read out loud to yourself, and one to send.

Journaling Space

Spend some time in prayer, asking God to help you move forward and to give your hurts and pains to him. He wants to carry them for you.

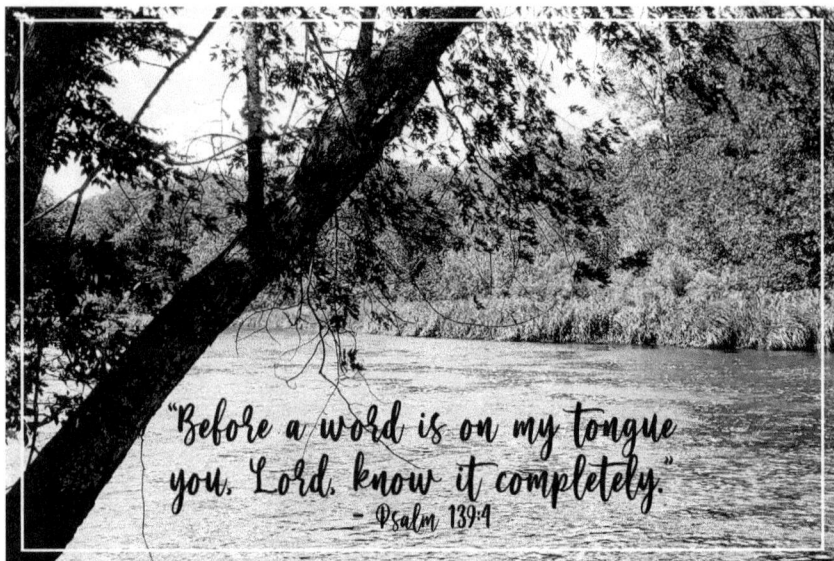

"Before a word is on my tongue you, Lord, know it completely."
— Psalm 139:4

"The past is the past if you let it stay there. Move forward with new beginnings!"

www.ingramcontent.com/pod-product-compliance
Lightning Source LLC
La Vergne TN
LVHW021540080426
835509LV00019B/2755

9 781637 651858